PERRIER GUIDE TO THE
CHINESE MENU

READER'S DIGEST

perrier

GUIDE TO THE

CHINESE

Contributor and adviser
Kenneth Lo

Contributing editor
Lizzie Boyd

PUBLISHED BY
THE READER'S DIGEST
ASSOCIATION LIMITED
LONDON NEW YORK MONTREAL
SYDNEY CAPE TOWN

Perrier/Reader's Digest Guide to the Chinese Menu was edited and designed by The Reader's Digest Association Limited, London

Printed in Great Britain

CONTENTS

FOREWORD

There are two problems which confront the European faced with a Chinese menu: firstly the size of the menu, which can be bewilderingly long, and secondly the format or pattern of a traditional meal. Any Chinese restaurant of repute will list some 100–200 dishes on its menu. While these dishes fall into the usual categories of starters, soups, meat, seafood, poultry, fish and dessert, a Chinese meal does not conform to the Western pattern of a soup or starter followed by a main course. In choosing dishes for a Chinese meal the procedure is to select a series of dishes and to eat them in groups like buffet dishes. Only at formal Chinese banquets are dishes served singly, course by course.

Starters are dishes meant only to be nibbled at, often crisp or savoury and spicy but always small enough merely to awaken the interest of the palate and encourage the appetite.

In a restaurant, the choice of starters ranges from conventional dishes such as Spare-Ribs, Crispy Prawns and Crispy Pancake Rolls to less common dishes like Stuffed Crab Claws, Snowflake Prawn Balls, Crispy Seaweeds, Cantonese Fresh-Poached Prawns in the Shells, Szechuan Bang Bang Chicken and Long-Braised Chicken Feet. From such an array of starters one will normally select two or three dishes as being adequate for a group of three or four people.

In the context of a Chinese meal, soup is not intended as a starter, as in a Western menu. It is a punctuation, breaking the sequel of different series of dishes and may be situated between starters and the 'big dishes' (whole fish, whole duck or chicken) or between the 'big dishes' and the concluding rice-accompanying dishes. At a family dinner where the

Kenneth Lo is the recognised authority on Chinese food. Author of numerous books, he appears frequently on TV and radio. He is also a director of a Chinese restaurant and cookery school.

majority of dishes are served more or less at once, soup is the centre point and spoonfuls are used to wash down mouthfuls of more solid food as the meal progresses. Such soups are usually clear, with finely shredded meat and vegetables; they are not exceptionally rich and tasty as these qualities are present in the solid foods, but they are always hot and refreshing, acting as a 'lubricant' and a digestive aid.

However, because of the difference between East and West in the concept of soups, those served at Chinese restaurants in the West have assumed a different role. Here it will be most suitable to have a soup between starters and main course dishes. The most common on the average menu are clear Egg Drop Soup, Wunton Soup and Fish Ball and Vegetable Soup, and thick Chicken and Sweet Corn Soup and Hot and Sour Soup. Off the beaten track are Shark's-Fin Soup and Bird's-Nest Soup, expensive though basically little different from other soups in body and savouriness.

After the soup follow correctly one or two meat dishes, to be succeeded in turn by a poultry dish, seafood, fish and a pure vegetable dish. In China, there are only two methods of cooking meat: quick stir-frying and long-cooking, either braised in soya sauce or steamed. Most restaurants are inclined to offer quick-fried dishes, but if possible choose one quick-fried meat dish and one long-cooked. Quick-fried Beef and Pimento in Black Bean Sauce, with an earthy flavour, could be contrasted with long-cooked pork such as Cantonese Braised Brisket of Beef or Shanghai Long-Cooked Knuckle of Pork. In a Pekingese restaurant choose Quick-Fried Sliced Lamb with Spring Onions in Garlic Sauce, which is typically Pekingese and almost invariably good.

Poultry dishes are either of the crispy-roasted or deep-fried types, or long-cooked and super tender. Peking Duck, Aromatic and Crispy Duck and Chopped Deep-Fried Eight Piece Chicken are in the crispy skin tradition. Eight Treasure Stuffed Duck and Cantonese Long-Braised Steamed Duck are tender ducks served in great sauces. In the majority of these poultry dishes, the birds are served whole and suitable therefore only for parties of six to eight or more people. Some, like Peking Duck, have to be timed precisely and must therefore be ordered in advance. For smaller parties the best poultry dishes are Peking Diced Chicken Cubes Quick-Fried in Yellow Bean Sauce or Szechuan Chilli Chicken.

Chinese cuisine is well known for its fish cookery and yet the only method distinctive to the Chinese is steaming. Fish is served with a variety of sauces or simply topped with freshly shredded onion and ginger and flamed with sizzling hot fat or oil. Steamed fish probably retains more natural taste and flavour than other cooking methods, and the larger the fish the better. Steamed whole fish is a luxury dish, usually available in the majority of good Cantonese restaurants and in some Pekingese establishments which regard it as a banquet dish.

There is a greater variety of seafood than of fish dishes on a Chinese menu. Prawns, shrimps, squid, scallop and crabs are particularly suitable for quick stir-frying, on their own or with other ingredients such as button mushrooms, peas, diced cucumber, celery or nuts, or in tomato, sweet and sour or black bean sauce or as *fu-yungs*, which means cooked in egg-white. They are also coated with batter and deep-fried; always appetising, they are usually better bets than corresponding fish dishes in restaurants and take-away shops of no particular reputation.

The problem of ordering from a Chinese menu, however large, can be reduced to selecting a couple of starters, one crisp and one spicy; a soup; two meat dishes (pork and/or beef); one or two seafood dishes (prawns and crab or lobster); and one vegetable dish. This number of dishes would be suitable for two to three people. For a party of four or five guests, order in addition a large fish dish and a whole-poultry dish. For larger numbers increase the starters by one or two items and double the size of their portions. Meat should be increased by one dish (and include lamb in a Pekingese restaurant), at least one of which should be a spicy meat dish from Szechuan. There would also be two seafood dishes, a large whole steamed fish and a minimum of one whole-poultry dish. The larger the party, the more sumptuous the occasion, which is how a Chinese meal is meant to be served.

Bamboo chopsticks are the traditional eating tools, invented by the Chinese while the rest of the world still used their fingers. Held between the fingers, chopsticks deftly transfer rice from bowl to mouth, pick out delicate morsels and firmly grip small joints. Some dexterity is called for, but on request restaurants will replace chopsticks with European cutlery. Rice wine and tea are the universal drinks of China; to Western palates sherry and dry white wines have that degree of delicacy which best flatters a Chinese meal.

STARTERS

The composition of a Chinese meal is a matter for great deliberation. It will consist of a number of dishes, upwards of five, which are all placed on the table simultaneously, except at large banquets where one series of dishes will follow another. Texture plays an important part, and some dishes will be crisp, in contrast to others which are quick-fried or long-steamed. Starters are an adaptation of Western-style menus, with emphasis on texture and delicacy of flavour. Spare ribs in soya sauce, deep-fried oysters or smoked fish which is not really smoked but marinated and dry-fried are served as starters.

1

2

1 CHINESE STARTERS
include such crisp delicacies
as *Won Tun* (far left), deep-
fried chicken dumplings,
next to *Cheung Gyun*, the
popular spring rolls. Left
are two Peking specialities:
Kan Pai Sung (crisp
seaweed) and *Chung Yiu
Ping* (crisp onion cake)

2 *Tai Pin Pan* (above) is
known as the Big-Platter
hors d'oeuvre and consists
of a selection of sliced
meats. Usually accom-
panied by rice wine

11

SOUPS

The Western concept of soup as a first course is unknown in Chinese cuisine. There is always at least one soup in a meal, and usually a second, often a sweet soup. They serve the dual functions of washing down dry foods and of clearing the palate of one flavour before progressing to the next. The majority of Chinese soups are crystal-clear consommé types with noodles or matchstick strips of meat, fish or vegetables. There are also thick soups-cum-stews such as spare rib and cabbage soup. Bird's-nest soup is flavoured with the residue of sea-swallows' nests and decorated with clouds of egg white.

1

4 Overleaf, from left: *Yu Tsi Tang* (shark's-fin soup), *Tou Fu Ha Rou Tang* (bean-curd and crab meat) and *Yien Wor Tang* (bird's-nest soup)

1 SOUPS, from left: *Hsi Hu Ngiu Keng Tang* (West Lake beef broth), *Chi Pien Tung Ku Tang* (chicken and mushroom soup) and *Chi Si Mein Tang* (chicken and noodles)

2 *Wan Ton* (clear soup with dumplings), *Suan La Tang* (hot and sour soup) and, below, *Rou Pien Bow Yu Tang* (abalone and pork soup)

3 *Ha Rou Si Mi Tang* (crab and sweet corn soup)

13

NOODLES

With rice, noodles are the ancient staple food of China; they are said to have been introduced to Italy by Marco Polo. There are various types, such as soup noodles and sauce noodles, associated with festive events, and *Wo Mein*, noodles cooked with other ingredients – in Cantonese cuisine often with prawns and crab – and chiefly found on restaurant menus. Fried noodles, with meat, vegetables and shellfish (*Chow Mein*) are the best known in the Western World, where they appear on every restaurant and take-away menu.

1 Mein: NOODLES
Four types of Chinese noodles are shown
Far left: *Lu Mein* (boiled noodles tossed in herb-flavoured sauce)
Top: *Wo Mein* (pot noodles northern style, cooked in meat sauce).
Right: *Cha Chiang Mein* (pot noodles Peking style, in meat sauce); and bottom *Chow Mein* (fried noodles)

2 Sing Jiu Mi Feng (above)
CHOW MEIN SINGAPORE STYLE
of quick-fried noodles with curry flavour

17

RICE

From time immemorial rice has been the staple, and often the only, food of China's millions, and served steamed, boiled or fried at every meal of the day. For breakfast, or as a late-night restorer and digestive aid, there is *Congee* of rice boiled in plenty of water to a soft-porridge consistency. The addition of meat, fish, vegetables and various condiments transforms *Congee* into the savoury, soft-rice dishes that are particular to the Cantonese cuisine. Fried rice is perhaps more to European tastes, simply as accompaniments or in various combinations.

EGG DISHES

1 3

2

1 Pi-Dan
   THOUSAND YEAR OLD EGGS
   cured in pine ashes and lime

2 Tseng Dan
   STEAMED BEATEN EGGS
   served with rice

Fu-Yung dishes on restaurant menus in the West are
egg dishes, though in China itself the same term is
applied only to delicate dishes of minced pork or
chicken beaten with egg whites. Most egg dishes are
of the scrambled or stir-fried type, blended with
savoury ingredients. Omelettes, usually filled, are
tiny and served with sweet-and-sour or meat sauce.
Yellow Flowing Eggs (*Liu Huang*) is a popular
Peking speciality of scrambled egg yolks. The
Thousand Year Old Eggs are mildly misnamed, as the
dish of pickled duck eggs are roughly 50 days young!

3 CHICKEN FU-YUNG
Miniature omelettes with
diced chicken and spring
onion filling; served with
plain boiled rice and a hot,
spicy sauce.

21

FISH AND SHELLFISH

Every kind of fish is eaten in China, and freshwater fish are as common and popular as saltwater types. For thousands of years fish farms stocked with carp and trout have been cultivated, and shrimps, crabs and lobsters are netted from vast inland waterways. Marinated fish is steamed or fried, but the *pièce de résistance* is large fish cooked whole, with savoury sauce ingredients of lily-bud stems, known as golden needles, water chestnuts and Chinese dried mushrooms. All types of shellfish are deep-fried; abalone, bland and rubbery, is rarely served on its own, but flavours soups, stews and fries.

1

1 Si Jiu Kuo Lung Ha
BLACK BEAN AND
CHILLI LOBSTER
Stir-fried lobster cooked in
soya and sherry-flavoured
sauce, with salted black
beans, garlic and chillis

2 Chiang Chung Kuo Ha
ONION AND GINGER CRAB
Crab pieces coated with
batter made with root
ginger and spring onions;
deep-fried and served with
hot dips

3 Kan Pien Ta Yu
WHOLE FISH IN REDUCED
BEAN PASTE AND DICED
PORK SAUCE
In Chinese cuisine, rich
meat sauces are typically
served with fish

4 Chi Ma Hsai
SESAME PRAWN TOASTS
Pounded prawns and
minced pork spread on
bread, dredged with sesame
seeds and deep-fried

5 Tseng Yu, Tsa Da Hsia
STEAMED WHOLE FISH AND
DEEP-FRIED CRISPY PRAWNS
the former marinated and
clear-steamed, the latter
coated with batter and fried
in hot oil

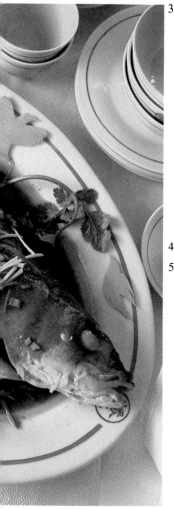

3

4
5

POULTRY

Chicken is popular and prepared in innumerable ways. Rubbed with garlic, ginger and soya sauce it is roasted to produce crisp skin and tender meat. Boiled, chopped into pieces and set in aspic it reappears as Crystal Chicken, and steeped in yellow wine it emerges as hors d'oeuvre in the name of Drunken Chicken. Duck is world famous in the classic preparation of Peking Duck, but there is also Eight-Precious Duck, so called after the eight ingredients, including rice, chestnuts, lotus seeds and bamboo shoots, which make up the stuffing. Poultry is also red-cooked: casserolled with ginger and soya sauce.

2

3

1 & 2 **Kao Ya**
PEKING DUCK
Crisp duck skin, aromatic
duck meat, spring onions
and cucumber are wrapped
in pancakes spread with
plum and hoisin sauces

3 Pa Ya (left)
STEAMED AND BRAISED
WHOLE DUCK

27

4

5

4 Yien Kuo Chi
   SALT-BAKED CHICKEN
   air-dried, buried whole in
   coarse sea salt and baked;
   chopped into small pieces
   for serving

5 Tsi-Bow Chi
   PAPER-WRAPPED CHICKEN
   seasoned chicken joints
   wrapped in paper and fried

6 Kuo Sao Ya
   CRISPY BONELESS DUCK
   coated with batter and
   deep-fried

7 Kam Ling
   CRISPY-SKIN, OIL-SPLASHED
   DUCK
   steamed, then double-fried,
   cut into pieces and served
   like Peking Duck

8   9

10

8 Ja Gai
DEEP-FRIED CRISPY CHICKEN
with prawn crackers

9 Kung-Pao Chi Ting
SZECHUAN QUICK-FRIED
DICED CHICKEN IN HOT
SAUCE
spicy chicken cubes

10 Mu-Koo Chi Pien
SLICED CHICKEN WITH
MUSHROOMS
quick-fried boned chicken

11 Chiang-Bow Chi Ting
PEKING QUICK-FRIED
DICED CHICKEN IN
SOYA-PASTE SAUCE

31

MEAT

Pork is by far the most common meat in China, eschewed only by the Moslems, who substitute it with beef or lamb dishes. Both pork and beef, inter-changeable in Chinese dishes abroad, are red-cooked, braised or roasted, but more often stir-fried. The meat is cut into matchstick shreds and quick-fried in vegetable oil and soya sauce, with, for example, bamboo shoots, bean sprouts, noodles, spring onions or mange-tout peas. The ingredients are tossed and scrambled over high heat for a few minutes, and the finished dish is the typical combination of tender aromatic meat and vegetables.

1

1 Ku Laow Rou
SWEET AND SOUR PORK
stir-fried with onion and
sweet peppers

2 Siu Yok
CANTONESE CRISPY-SKIN
PORK
roast pork, the crackling
crisped with spices, soya
sauce and honey.

3 Cha Siu Rou
CANTONESE BARBECUED
PORK
roasted in oil, sherry, honey,
soya and hoisin sauces

4 Pai Ku
BARBECUED SPARE RIBS
braised in oil, sherry and
soya sauce, with black
beans, garlic and ginger

3

4

5

6

7

5 Si-Jeow Ngiu Rou
QUICK-FRIED BLACK BEAN
CHILLI BEEF

6 Hao Yiu Ngiu Rou
QUICK-FRIED BEEF IN WINE
AND OYSTER SAUCE

7 Yang Chung Chow Ngiu
Rou
QUICK-FRIED SHREDDED BEEF

8 Ka Shao Ngiu Rou Si
SZECHUAN HOT-FRIED CRISPY
SHREDDED BEEF

9 Ngiu Nan
CANTONESE LONG-BRAISED
BEEF

10 Ching Jiew Ngiu Rou
QUICK-FRIED BEEF RIBBONS
WITH GREEN PEPPERS

8

9

10

11

12

13

11 Shao Yang Rou
BARBECUED SLICED LAMB
often grilled at the table
and served with dips.
Peking speciality

12 Chung Pao Yang Rou
QUICK-FRIED LAMB WITH
SPRING ONIONS
marinated in soya sauce,
sherry, ginger and garlic

13 Suan Yang Rou
MONGOLIAN LAMB HOT-POT
of Mongolian origin, now a
Peking speciality, always
cooked at the table.
Chinese leaves and
cabbage, with thin lamb
slices, are briefly cooked in
a pot of boiling stock then
dipped into sauces – soya,
hoisin, chilli and sesame

VEGETABLES

3

Most vegetable and vegetarian dishes have
originated in Buddhist monasteries; stir or quick-
fried they are often blended with other ingredients
for contrasting texture and flavour. Popular dishes
include whole spinach fried in oil flavoured with
ginger, garlic and onion and finished off in soya
sauce and stock; Fu-Yung cauliflower is fried with
minced chicken and topped with ham. The Eight
Precious Hot Salad consists of lily-bud stems,
Chinese wood ears (a fungus) and dried mushrooms,
bean curds, carrots and turnips, bamboo shoots,
celery and bean sprouts, all stir-fried.

1

2

1 Tien Suan Bai Tsai
SWEET AND SOUR CHINESE
CABBAGE
stir-fried with soya sauce,
orange juice and sugar

2 Lo-Han
QUICK-FRIED MIXED FRESH
AND DRIED VEGETABLES
known poetically as
Buddhist's Delight

3 Chow Laing Tou
QUICK-FRIED MANGE TOUT
cooked in oil, lard and
chicken stock

4 Chow Suen Tung
QUICK-FRIED CHINESE
MUSHROOMS AND BAMBOO
SHOOTS
with dried, reconstituted
black mushroom caps

4

SWEETS AND FRUIT

Over thousands of years the Chinese have used their unequalled artistic flair in perfecting savoury dishes of great delicacy. Perhaps their imagination gave out when it came to desserts or perhaps sweet ingredients are used so extensively in savoury food that there is no need to pamper to a sweet tooth. Whatever the reason, there is no dessert course to a Chinese meal, though restaurants cater for Western-style habits and offer a few sweet dishes as well as ice creams and fruit salads. Fresh fruit may in season include juicy, sweet and aromatic lychees, sour-sweet loquats, mangosteens and pomegranates.

1

2

1 Pa-Si Ping-Kuo
PEKING TOFFEE APPLES
of deep-fried apple fritters
coated with brittle sugar
caramel

2 Hsing Ren Tou Fou
ALMOND CURD JUNKET
of ground almonds and rice
jelly in syrup decorated
with glacé cherries

3 Tea (overleaf) is served with
reverent ceremony, poured
into thin cups whose design
has remained unchanged
over thousands of years.
Keemun, with a rich smoky
aroma, or the green *Loong
Ching* are served with most
foods. Jasmine-scented tea
has an incomparably
delicate flavour

DIM SUM

SAVOURY DIM SUM
include (top row, left) *Cheung Fun* (stuffed rice-flour rolls),
Gai Pau (steamed chicken buns), *Chi Ma Hsia* (sesame
prawn toasts) and, below, *Cha Siu Pau* (steamed pork

Between meals the Chinese frequent tea houses to sample a variety of snacks known collectively as *Dim Sum*. Most are savoury and arrive at the table in round bamboo containers, with saucers of dips and pickles. There are small boiled, steamed or fried pastry dumplings, plain or stuffed with meat, shellfish or vegetables, and there are stuffed, deep-fried pancakes. Especially popular are large, steamed yeast buns with sweet or savoury fillings. Plain buns like *Hua Chuan* accompany meat dishes, like bread rolls in Western restaurants.

buns). Second row: *Siu Mai* (open pork dumplings), *Lin Yung Pau* (steamed lotus seed buns), *Fun Kuo* (fried prawn dumplings); below, *Har Kau* (steamed prawn dumplings)

Among the more unusual
DIM SUM are (top) *Woo Kok*
(crisp-fried yam croquettes
stuffed with minced meat).
Below are sweet *Ma Ti Kao*
(squares or fingers of water
chestnut jelly) and *Dan Ta*
(Cantonese egg custard
tartlets)

GLOSSARY OF CHINESE MENU AND CULINARY TERMS

The Cantonese cuisine is the best known in the Western World; the following headwords are therefore listed according to Cantonese spelling, followed by the Mandarin word (in brackets) where an equivalent exists.

B

Baan (Pao): a North China form for quick-frying whereby in the second phase the finely cut food is rapidly stir-fried over high heat, either in a thickened sauce or in flavoured oil.

Bau (Bao): steamed buns.

Beef Cheung-Fan: steamed rice-flour rolls stuffed with beef; a savoury DIM SUM.

Boot Gok (Ba Jiao): anise or star anise, a star-shaped seed capsule with a pungent flavour; essential in Chinese cooking and known also as the eight point.

Bow Yee (Bau Yu): abalone, an ivory-coloured, rubbery shellfish.

C

Chaan (Chao): general term for stir-frying or quick-frying.

Cha Siu (Cha Shao): Cantonese method of quick barbecue roasting where chunks of marinated meat are subjected to short periods of roasting over high heat.

Cha Siu Baau: type of DIM SUMS, steamed buns stuffed with CHA SIU roast pork.

Cha Siu Cheung-Fan: similar to above, but in steamed rice-flour rolls.

Cheung Gyun: crisp spring rolls. See also Cantonese Specialities.

Choo (Cu): vinegar.

D

Daan Ta Gou: sweet DIM SUMS; egg custard.

Dahn (Dun): slow steaming in a closed receptacle or double boiler.

Dauh Sa Baau: steamed DIM SUMS stuffed with sweet bean paste.

Deem Sums (Dian Xin): another name for small savoury snacks (DIM SUMS).

Dim Sums: collective term for small savoury or sweet snacks, usually served in Chinese tea houses throughout the day, as light meals and as accompaniments to drinks.

Don (Dan): egg.

Doon Guar (Dong Gua): vegetable marrow.

Dow Foo (Dou Fu): bean curd.

Dow Gna (Dou Ya): bean sprouts.

Dow Sa (Dou Sha): sweet

ground beans.

Dow See (Douchi): black beans, salted and fermented.

Doy Koo (Dong Gu): Chinese black dried mushrooms. Also known as winter mushrooms.

F

Faat Choy: hairy type of edible seaweed.

Fan (Xun): smoking (of food); also cooked (of rice); Mandarin: Fan.

Fung (Feng): drying, i.e. wind-drying of meat and poultry.

G

Gai Jat: savoury DIM SUMS of chicken meat rolled in bean-curd skin.

H

Ha Gow: steamed DIM SUMS stuffed with prawns.

Har Peen (Xia Pian): shrimp or prawn chips.

Hom Dom (Xian Dan): salt egg.

Hong (Hong): grilling.

Ho Yo (Hau You): oyster sauce.

Hua Chuan is the Chinese version of a dinner roll and invariably offered in restaurants as an accompaniment to rich dishes. Also known as flower rolls, the small, raised, open-ended yeast buns are steamed and served hot. They are a refined type of *Maahn Tauk* (or *Man Tou*) buns, an essential bulk food in north China equalling rice in importance and eaten hot for breakfast, lunch and dinner.

Hwa (Xie): crab.

J

Ja (Zha): deep-frying.

Jee Ma You (Zhi Ma Yiu): sesame oil.

Jeui (Zui): Marinating in wine or spirits.

Jeung (Jiang): prolonged seasoning in salted soya bean paste.

Jeung Yow: soya sauce.

Ji Bou Gai: savoury DIM SUMS of paper-wrapped deep-fried chicken.

Ji Bou Ha: similar to the above, but deep-fried prawns in steamed buns.

Jin (Jian): shallow-frying.

Jing (Zheng): open or wet steaming, with the food being subjected to the direct action of steam.

Jing Don (Zheng Dan): steamed savoury eggs.

Jing Yuk Paaih: steamed pork-rib chops.

Jook Jun (Zhu Jun): bamboo shoots.

Ju: pork.

Juk (Zhou): soft rice or congee.

Jyu (Zhu): plain boiling.

K

Kan Siu (Kan Bien): dry-braising, a process of quick-frying where the sauce in which the food is cooked is rapidly reduced over high heat.

Kau (Kou): applied to a steamed dish which, like a steamed pudding, is turned out on to a dish before serving.

Kow (Kao): roasting or baking.

L

La Chuan Kuen: Cantonese sausage roll, type of DIM SUMS.

Lah Jew Jeong: hot chilli sauce.

Lam (Lin): splash-frying, by ladling hot oil over food suspended over a pan of boiling oil.

Lau (liu): soft food, especially fish, quick-fried in a thickened sauce without the usual stirring.

Lin Gee (Lianzi): lotus seeds.

Lihn Yohng Baau: sweet DIM SUMS of steamed buns stuffed with lotus seed paste.

Loh Baahk Gou: turnip DIM SUMS.

Loong Ngon (Long Yan): dragon eye fruit.

Lou (Lu): slow cooking in soya sauce.

Lung Har (Long Xia): lobster.

M

Ma La Gou: sponge cake, sweet DIM SUMS.

Mah Tai: water chestnuts.

Mah Tai Gou: sweet DIM SUMS of water chestnut cake.

Man (Men): long, slow cooking over low heat.

May Fun (Mi Fen): rice-flour noodles.

Mein (Mian): noodles.

Min Seeh: soya bean jam.

Mook Yee (Mu Er): wood ear fungi (mushrooms).

N

Ngaap Geuk Jat: DIM SUMS; long-braised duck's feet wrapped and steamed in bean-curd skins.

Ngo Maih Gai: savoury rice wrapped in lotus leaves.

Ngow Yuk (Niu Rou): beef.

O

Opp (Ya): duck.

P

Pao, as a prefix, describes rapid cooking over high heat either in oil (*Yiu Pao*) or in stock (*Tang Pao*). Literally meaning explosion, it is the last stage in any cooking process which can include steaming, shallow or deep-frying.

Pay Don (Pi Dan): hundred year old eggs. See also Pekingese specialities.

Q

Quar Gee (Qua Zi): melon seeds.

S

Sang Geung (Sheng Jiang): root ginger.
See You (Jian You): soya sauce.
Shuen Mooey (Suan Mei Jiang): plum sauce.
Si Guar (Shi Guar): water melon.
Siu (Shao): stewing or braising.
Siu Mai: steamed DIM SUMS, stuffed with meat, open-topped.

T

Tim Shuan (Tian Suan): sweet and sour.

W

Wu Gok: DIM SUMS of mashed yam balls stuffed with minced meat.
Wui (Hui): Blending several types of foods and ingredients in the final phase of cooking.

Y

Yihm (Yan): salting or preserving in salt.
Yin Wor (Yan Wo): bird's nest.
Young (Niang): stuffed.
Yo Yee (You Yu): squid.
Yuh Chi Baau: large steamed dumpling stuffed with shark's fin.

Yu Chee, or shark's fin, has a sticky, jelly-like texture. Purchased dried and rock-hard it needs long soaking and cooking. Offered only at expensive restaurants.

CANTONESE SPECIALITIES

B

Baahk Jam Gai: white cut chicken (lightly boiled chicken chopped into bite-size pieces).

Baahk Pin Yuhk: white cut pork (usually belly of pork boiled until just tender, then cut into thin slices and served with dips).

Baat Bou Ap: eight-treasure duck (stuffed with eight ingredients and usually long-steamed until tender enough to be dismembered at the table with chopsticks.

Baat Bou Faahn: eight-treasure rice (banquet or party dish of sweet steamed rice pudding, studded with coloured glacé fruits).

Baat Bou Gai: eight-treasure chicken (chicken stuffed with eight ingredients, e.g. chestnuts, Chinese dried mushrooms, rice, bamboo shoots, smoked ham, lotus seeds, lily-bud stems and shrimps. Steamed and served whole).

Baau Yuh Wuih Seung Dung: braised abalone with winter mushrooms and bamboo shoots. Considered a delicacy for party menus.

Bauh Haahm Yuh Siu Yuhk: red-cooked pork with abalone and salted fish.

Bauh Yuh Gai Tong: abalone and chicken soup.

Bau Ji: steamed buns with a variety of fillings, such as pork, chicken, vegetables, sweet lotus seeds or sweet bean paste.

C

Chaau (Chow) is a popular frying process at restaurants and take-away establishments. It is accomplished in a few minutes and known as stir or quick-frying. The food, cut into strips or thin slices, is fried in a small amount of oil and, like our scrambled eggs, kept in constant movement on the pan until hot and coated with the oil and seasoning.

Chaau Bok Choi: stir-fried Chinese celery cabbage, also called Chinese leaf.

Chaau Choi: general term for stir-fried vegetables.

Chaau Faahn: fried rice.

Chaau Gai Dan: stir-fried eggs, the Chinese equivalent of scrambled eggs which are

only lightly beaten and stirred in the pan.

Chaau Mihn: fried noodles, also called Chow Mein.

Chaau Suen Dong: quick-fried and braised 'Two Winters' (bamboo shoots and mushrooms).

Cha Siu Yuhk: quick-baked, marinated pork (fillet of pork roasted over high heat; served cut into thin slices).

Cheung Gyun: spring rolls. Served in China as pancakes with a variety of stuffings for the diners to wrap up their own rolls; outside China, spring rolls are usually served stuffed, fried and crisp.

Ching Chaau Ha Yahn: quick-fried prawns (seasoned with salt and ginger and quick-fried in oil and stock).

Ching Jing Yuh: steamed fish; usually an outstanding dish in reputable restaurants.

Ching Tong Gap Leih: steamed clams.

Chow Mein: see Chaau Mihn.

Chung Maih Gon Pin: onion-cooked sliced liver.

Chung Shao Ap: duck stuffed with onion and cooked whole.

D

Da Pien Lou: A so-called hot pot, cooked at table in a chafing dish in the manner of a Swiss fondue. Da Pien Lou

is a refined version of SAAN YEUHNG YUHK, with the addition of sliced fish, prawns, abalone, mushrooms, bamboo shoots and sometimes lobster. In Hong Kong and Singapore it is popularly known as Steamboat.

Dauh Gu Chaau Yauh Yuh: quick-fried squid in black bean paste.

Dauh Gu Gai: chicken pieces stir-fried in black bean sauce.

Dong Gu Siu Dou Fou: soya-braised bean curd.

Dou Foo Boi Choi Tang: bean curd and spinach soup.

F

Fuhng Meih Ha is one of the favourite Cantonese dishes with Westerners. It consists of giant prawns, shelled except for the tails, which when fried turn bright red and explain the common name of Phoenix-tail prawns. Coated with batter, the prawns are deep-fried in oil, piled on a dish and served with a bowl of fried sea salt and pepper and a garlic and ginger-flavoured soya sauce dip. The tails make convenient handles.

Fan Gai: seasoned chicken, steamed then smoked.

Fu Yuhng Gai Pin: sliced, quick-fried chicken in egg-white sauce.

G

Gaai Sih Chaau Mihn: chicken and fried noodles.

Gaai Uuht ap Jeung: ducks' feet in mustard sauce; slow-cooked and served cold as an hors d'oeuvre.

Gai Faahn: chicken and fried rice.

Gai Si Tong Mihn: chicken noodle soup.

Gai Tong: chicken soup.

Gau Gei Nganh Bin Tong: soup cum stew of tangerine-flavoured, long-cooked ox penis; the dish occasionally appears on Chinese restaurant menus.

Geung Chung Wo Haaih: onion and ginger crab; popular Cantonese dish. See below.

Geung Chung Wo Luhng Ha: onion and ginger lobster (quick-fried lobster chunks braised with ginger and onion in stock, wine and soya sauce). Crab is cooked in the same way.

Guk Fa Wo: chrysanthemum hot-pot, a version of DA PIEN LOU. The hot-pot is assembled in the kitchen, with a variety of cooked and raw ingredients and brought to the table flaming like petals of chrysanthemum.

Gwong Dun Siu Ap: a general term for Cantonese roast duck – the shiny brown, lacquered duck seen hanging in the windows of Cantonese restaurants.

H

Haaih Wohng Yuh Chi: shark's fin braised with crab meat and crab eggs.

Haaih Yuhk Chaau Gai Dan: stir-fried (scrambled) eggs with crab meat.

Hahng Yahn Chah almost approaches the European idea of a sweet. Known as almond tea, it is made from ground rice and almonds, sweetened and blended with water. It resembles a runny custard and is served hot in small bowls, as a snack or at the end of a meal.

Hahng Yahn Dauh Fuh: jelly made from almond tea, set and cut into cubes; served with fruit salads.

Hau Yiu Chaau Gai Lan Choi: quick-fried broccoli in oyster sauce.

Ha Yuehk Su Mi Tong; crab and sweet corn soup.

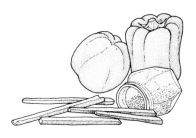

Ha Yuehk Pa Bok Choi: braised Chinese cabbage with crab meat.

Houh Yauh Ngauh Yuhk: sliced beef in oyster sauce.

Huhng Siu Baau Yuh: braised abalone.

Huhng Siu Dou Fou: soya-braised bean curd.

Huhng Siu Jyu Touh: red-cooked tripe.

Huhng Siu Jyu Yuhk: red-cooked pork (belly of pork long-braised in soya sauce).

Huhng Siu Ngauh Ngaan: red-cooked brisket of beef, usually served in metal casserole dish.

Huhng Siu Ngauh Touh: red-cooked ox tripe.

Huhng Siu Paaih Gwat: red-cooked spare ribs.

Huhng Siu Yuh: red-cooked fish.

Huhng Siu Yuh Chi: red-cooked shark's fin (shark's fins, except in soups, are extremely expensive).

J

Ja Gai: fried crispy chicken (fried whole, served chopped into pieces).

Jeui Gai: drunken chicken (steeped with ginger and onions in dry sherry for at least 2 days; served in bite-size pieces as cold hors d'oeuvre).

Ji Beau Gai: paper-wrapped chicken (small joints wrapped and fried in cellophane paper).

Jing Dan: steamed eggs (beaten eggs blended with stock and steamed like a savoury custard).

Juk: soft rice, also known as congee; cooked in plenty of water, to a soup-like consistency.

K

Kau Yukk: pork pudding.

Kow Ji: steamed dough dumplings stuffed with prawns or minced meat.

L

Lo-Han Pa Ap: whole duck braised with mixture of dried and fresh vegetables.

Loh Hon Choi: The Buddhist Vegetable Ensemble (fresh and dried vegetables, cooked and arranged as traditional in Buddhist temples and monasteries.

M

Maahn Tauh: steamed bread rolls. See also Hua Chuan.

N

Neugn Dung Gu: stuffed and braised mushrooms.

Ngauh Yuhk Si Chaau Yehng Chung: quick-fried beef with onions.

Ngh Lauh Yuh: five willow fish (sweet and sour fish cooked and garnished with five shredded vegetables).

Ngoh Maih Faahn: steamed rice wrapped in lotus leaves.

P

Pan Mihn: boiled noodles, often served as a cold starter tossed with diced chicken and vegetables.

S

Saan Yeuhng Yuhk: Cantonese name for Peking hot-pot (Shuan Yang Rout). See also DA PIEN LOU.

Sai Gwa Jung: water-melon pond (hollowed-out water melon filled with diced fruit).

Sai Hung Chih Chaau Gai Dan: stir-fried (scrambled) eggs with tomatoes.

Shuan Yang Rout: Mandarin for Peking hot-pot; see also SAAN YEUHNG YUHK and DA PIEN LOU.

Si Jiu Kuo Ha: stir-fried crab meat with salted black beans, garlic, green peppers, ginger and onions.

Siu Maai: steamed dough dumplings, open at the top to reveal the savoury stuffing.

Siu Ya: roast duck, stuffed with liquid filling of garlic, onion, parsley and star anise with oil, sherry and soya sauce. Basted with honey and vinegar and served with the thickened pan juices.

Siu Yuh Jyu: roast sucking pig.

Sou Sahp Gam: mixture of stir-fried vegetables.

Sub-Gum Chaau Mihn: noodles stir-fried with a variety (theoretically ten) of shredded ingredients.

T

Tien-Shun Pai-Ku: small pork spare ribs stir-fried in sweet and sour sauce.

Tim Syun Ap: sweet and sour sliced duck.

Tit Wo Dan: literally iron-pot or grown eggs, i.e. small soufflés, with various flavours.

Tohng Chou Gu Lou Tuhk: sweet and sour pork.

Tohng Chou Jyu Taih: sweet and sour pig's trotters.

Tohng Chou Paaih Gwat: sweet and sour spare ribs.

Tohng Chou Yuh: sweet and sour fish; may be served whole or filleted and cut into slices.

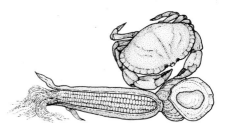

Tong Mihn: soup noodles.

W

Wahn Tan Tong: won ton soup.

Waht Yuh Yuhn: fish ball soup cum stew.

> **Wo Mein,** frequently seen on Cantonese menus, vies with *Chow Mein* in popularity. The latter are stir-fried while *Wo Mein* egg noodles are pot-cooked in a sauce. They are served up on a dish and lavishly garnished with shredded vegetables, prawns, crab or lobster meat.

Y

Yihm Wo Gai: whole chicken baked in salt; served chopped into pieces.

Yin Wo Tong: bird's-nest soup.

Yuh Chi Tong: shark's-fin soup.

Yuhk Pin Wohng Gwa Tong: sliced pork and cucumber soup.

Yuhk Sih Chaau Mihn: stir-fried noodles topped with lily-bud stems, bean sprouts and shredded pork.

Yuhk Yuhn Boi Choi Tong: meat balls and spinach soup.

Yuhn Siu Gwat Ji Gang: tangerine soup with small rice dumplings (clear soup flavoured with tangerine juice; the dumplings are filled with a mixture of sugar, sesame seeds and pork fat).

PEKINGESE AND SZECHUAN SPECIALITIES

B

Ba Bao Fan: eight-treasure rice; the equivalent of the Cantonese BAAT BOU FAAHN.

Ba Bao Ji: eight-treasure chicken; see Cantonese BAAT BOU GAI.

Ba Bao Ya: eight-precious duck; a party dish and so named after the eight or more stuffing ingredients. These include barley and rice, chestnuts, lotus seeds and ginkgo nuts, bamboo shoots, roast pork and smoked ham. Long-simmered in a casserole with spring onions, ginger, stock, soya sauce and sherry until the meat is so tender it falls from the bones.

Ba Ya: long-braised, steamed duck.

Ba Si Ping Guo: toffee apples, also known as Peking brittle-glazed apples.

Bai Pian Rou: white cut pork (thinly sliced, boiled pork, served cold with soya sauce, garlic and vinegar dips).

Bai Shao Bai Cai: braised Chinese cabbage.

Bao Yu Chao Shuang Dong: braised abalone with dried mushrooms and winter mushrooms.

Bing Tang Yin: silver ear in crystal sugar soup (a dessert soup with white wood ear, a type of fungus).

C

Cai Fan: rice boiled with vegetables.

Chaang Shiu Mian: long-life noodles in egg sauce; in China eggs are associated with a long life, and the dish is traditional at birthdays.

Cha An: tea or marbled eggs (hard-boiled with tea leaves).

Cha Pa Kuai: crisp-fried chicken, chopped into eight pieces for serving.

Cha Sha Ya: barbecued duck (dried duck, grilled on the spit, served with pancakes like Peking duck).

Cha Shao Ji: Moslem barbecued chicken (stuffed chicken grilled on the spit).

Cha Siu Fan: rice served with roast pork.

Cha Wan Zi: deep-fried, crisp pork balls.

Chao Cai: general term for stir-fried vegetables.

Chao Cai Hua: quick-fried cauliflower.

Chao Dou Jeu: quick-fried French beans.

Chao Dou Ya: quick-fried bean sprouts.

Chao Fan: basic fried rice, first boiled then stir-fried in oil with diced vegetables, ham, scrambled eggs and soya sauce.

Chao Gai Laan: braised broccoli.

Chao Ho Laing Dou: quick-fried snow peas (mange-touts).

Chao Kan Pian: quick-fried sliced pig's liver.

Chao Mian: fried noodles; also called Chow Mein.

Chao Po Tsai: spinach quick-fried with onions, garlic and root ginger in oil, lard, stock, soya sauce and sherry; cooked over high heat the spinach retains a glossy green colour.

Chao San Xian: stir-fried squid with prawns and diced pork.

Chao Yang Rou Pian: quick-fried sliced lamb.

Chao Ya Tsai: stir-fried bean sprouts with onions, garlic and ginger

Chi Si Ying Er Tang: sweet soup of shredded chicken and silver ear mushrooms (white fungi, dried and reconstituted before use).

Ching Chao Xia Reb: quick-

fried prawns with snow pickles.

Ching Dun Ji Tang: whole chicken soup; a clear soup drunk before the chicken is taken to pieces with chopsticks.

Ching Dun Ya Tang: whole duck soup; as above, but made with duck.

Ching Zheng Long Xia: steamed lobster.

Chou Jiac Yu Pian Tang: sliced fish pepper-pot soup.

Chow Mein: see Chao Mian.

D

Dan Dan Mian: Szechuan noodles tossed in hot meat sauce.

Dan Hwa Tang: egg-flower soup.

Dong Po Yang Rou: Tung-Po braised lamb with carrots, onion, peppercorns and wine; said to have been invented by the Sung Dynasty poet, Soo Tung-Po.

Dong Sun Shao Rou: Red-cooked pork with winter bamboo shoots.

Dou Ya Chao Rou Si: quick-fried shredded pork with bean sprouts.

F

Fan: boiled rice.
Fei Chang Dou Sha Tang: Szechuan pork tripe and green pea soup.

Feng Si Chao Sou Cai: stir-fried mixture of pea-starch transparent noodles and vegetables.

Feng Wei Xia: Phoenix-tail prawns; see Cantonese FUHNG MEIH HA.

Fu-Yung: cooking preparation of minced chicken, cornflour and egg white, used extensively in stir-fried dishes.

Fu-Yung Bian Duo: Fu-Yung broad beans.

Fu-Yung Cai Hua: Fu-Yung cauliflower.

Fu-Yung Ji: chicken Fu-Yung.

Fu-Yung Tsai Hua: stir-fried cauliflower florets in minced chicken and egg-white sauce.

Fu-Yung Yu Pian: Fu-Yung sliced fish.

G

Gan Bei Rou Pian Long Xu Cai Tang: dried scallop and sliced meat soup with asparagus.

Gan Bian Niu Rou Si: Szechuan dry-fried shredded beef with shredded celery, the beef fried crisp and coated in a hot reduced sauce.

Gan Chao Da Xia: dry-fried giant prawns in reduced sauce.

Gao Tang: clear soup or stock.

Gong Bao Ji Ding: Szechuan

diced pork cubes quick-fried with hot chilli oil.

Gong Bao Yao Kuai: quick-fried strips of kidney decorated with wood ear fungi.

Gui Fei Ji: Royal concubine chicken, a Shanghai invention of chopped chicken pieces first fried with mushrooms and bamboo shoots, then cooked in wine.

Guo Shao Ya: crisp boneless duck pieces, coated with batter and deep-fried.

H

He To Lou: sweet walnut soup.

Hong Shao Bai Cai: braised Chinese cabbage with soya sauce.

Hong Shao Bao Yu: red-cooked abalone.

Hong Shao Niu Rou: red-cooked beef.

Hong Shao Yang Rou: red-cooked lamb. This and red-cooked beef are slow-braised in soya sauce and served in bowls or casseroles.

Hong Shao Yu: soya-braised fish.

Hong Shao Yu Chi: red-cooked shark's fin.

Hseuh Cai Rou Shi Tang Mian: soup noodles with shredded pork and pickles.

Hsiang Jiu Kuo Zha: banana fritters.

Hui Gao Rou: Szechuan double cooked pork, first boiled, then sliced and quick-fried in hot sauce.

Hui Liang Ji Si: quick-fried mixture of two types of chicken: shredded fresh chicken stir-fried with shredded smoked or soya-braised chicken.

Hung Shao Ji: red-cooked chicken, braised in soya.

J

Ja Chiang Mian: Peking noodles tossed with meat sauce and shredded vegetables

Jaow Liu Yu Pian: soft-fried sliced fish in wine sauce.

Jiang Cong Guo Da Xia: onion and ginger quick-braised crab.

Jiao Zha Yang Rou: North Yangtse deep-fried crispy lamb; first braised, then coated with batter, deep-fried until crisp and sliced before serving.

Ji Bao Chi: chicken stuffed with shark's fin.

Ji Fan: rice with chicken.

Jin Pai Yuo Ji: gold coin chicken (steeped in stock until golden-brown, then cut into thin round slices and arranged like coins on a serving dish.)

Ji Pien Dung Gu Tang: Chinese mushroom and sliced chicken soup.

Ji Shi Chao Mian: fried noodles with shredded chicken.

Ji Tang: chicken soup or broth.

Ju Sa Tou Fu: coral bean curd.

Ju Kuai-z: bamboo chopsticks, the eating tools which the Chinese handle with dexterity.

K

Kao Ya, better known as Peking duck, has gained a worldwide reputation, due in no small measure to the elegant presentation of the dish and the ceremony attached to eating it. It is accompanied by small side dishes of bottle-brush spring onions and crisp strips of cucumber, and bowls of plum, hoisin and soya sauces. There is a plate heaped with puffy, steam-fried pancakes (*Bao Pin*) which become receptacles for the sauces and spring onions, the cracklingly crisp duck skin and the tender meat. The pancakes, rolled up round this delicious filling and eaten with the fingers, are an unforgettable meal.

Kue-Ta Tou Fu: braised bean curd in egg batter.

Kui Kuo Rou Ting: quick-fried pork with cashew nuts.

Kung Po Ji Ding: Szechuan diced chicken stir-fried in hot sauce.

L

Len Pan Ji Shi: cooked, shredded chicken tossed in a sauce; served cold as an hors d'oeuvre.

Liu Huang: literally yellow flowing eggs of beaten egg yolks stir-fried in oil and lard until glossy.

Li-zi Fen: 'Peking Dust', dessert of meringue coated with powdered chestnuts.

Long Zia Zheng Dan: lobster steamed with egg.

Lou Mian: noodles cooked in meat sauce.

Luo Han Cai: The Buddhist Vegetable Ensemble; see Cantonese LOH HON CHOI.

M

Mian: Noodles.

Mi Fen Zheng Rou: long-steamed pork in ground rice which is often roasted first to impart aroma to the meat.

Mi Tang Zheng Li: poached pears with honey and liqueur syrup.

Mu Shu Rou: shredded pork

quick-fried with wood-ear fungi and stir-fried eggs.

N

Niu Rou Shi Chao Mian: fried noodles with shredded beef.
Niu Rou Si Chao Yang Cong: quick-fried beef with onions.

P, Q

Pei-fing Kao Ya: another name for Kao Ya.
Pi Dan: thousand year old eggs – duck eggs sealed in a coating of pine ash and lime, left for 50 days to mature, then cleaned and shelled to reveal a yellow-green colour and pungent cheesy aroma. Also called Song Hua.
Quing Zheng Yu: clear steamed fish.

R

Rou Si Tza Chai Tang: soup of pork and shredded Szechuan pickle, a pungent salted cabbage strongly flavoured with red chilli pepper.

S

San Xian Tang: triple fresh ingredient soup of chicken, mushrooms and bamboo shoots.

Sha Guo Yu Chi: casserole of shark's fin.
Shao Chieh Zi: braised aubergines.
Shao Niang Dong Gu: braised stuffed mushrooms.
Shao Niang Huang Gua: braised stuffed cucumber.
Shao Ru Zhu: crisp roast sucking pig.
Shao San Sou: braised three vegetables, always containing bamboo shoots and mushrooms, with one other.
Shao Sou Cai: general term for braised vegetables.
Shao Tou Fu: braised bean curd.
Shao Yang Rou: famous Chinese–Moslem dish of sliced lamb cooked at table. See illustration on p. 36.
Shih -Jing Chao Mian: fried noodles with a variety of shredded ingredients.
Shih Jing Hui Mian: braised noodles with various other ingredients.
Shing Hung Shi Chao Ji Dan: stir-fried eggs with tomato.
Shi Zi Tou: braised lion's head meat balls, made from minced pork with water chestnuts, onions and Chinese fried mushrooms. Served with stir-fried spinach and noodles.
Shui Zhu Hiu Rou: long-simmered beef; popular Chinese–Moslem dish.
Song Hua: see PI DAN.

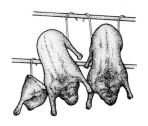

Sou He Guo: vegetarian hot-pot.

Suan La Tang: hot and sour soup. A north China speciality of thick soup made with shredded pork, dried mushrooms, bean curd, bamboo shoots, soya sauce and vinegar.

T, W

Tang Chu Yu Pian: soft-fried sliced fish in sweet and sour sauce.

Tang Mian: soup noodles.

Tang Zheng Rou: seasoned pork, steamed with brown sugar.

Tou Sa Kuo Ping: pancake rolls stuffed with sweet black or red bean purée.

Tsao Liu Yu Pien: fish fillets in white wine sauce.

Wu Liu Yu: five-willow fish, i.e. cooked with five different shredded ingredients.

X

Xia Ren Chao Ji Dan: stir-fried eggs with shrimps.

Xian Dan: soft-boiled eggs marinated in salt and soya sauce; breakfast dish.

Xiang Su Ya: Szechuan aromatic and crispy duck.

Xi Hong Shi Huang Men Niu Rou: braised beef with tomatoes.

Xun Ji: smoked chicken.

Xun Yu: smoked fish.

Y

Ya Fan: rice served with duck.

Yang Gao: jellied lamb, a cold hors d'oueuvre.

Yan Wo Tang: bird's-nest soup.

Yi Pin Guo: First-Rank Hot-pot; the Peking equivalent to Cantonese GUK FA WO.

You Yu Chao Ching Jiao: quick-fried squid with green pepper.

Yuan Bao Rou: red-cooked pork with boiled eggs.

Yu Chi Tang: shark's-fin soup.

Yu Lin Ji: oil-basted chicken; suspended over hot oil and basted until cooked.

Yu Mi Xia Rou Tang: sweet corn and crab meat soup.

Z

Zha Niu Li Ji: deep-fried, crisp, salted and peppered, shredded beef.

Zha Xie: deep-fried crab.

Zhang Cha Xun Ya: marinated duck smoked over camphor wood and tea leaves.

Zi Jiang Chao Ya Si: quick-fried ribbons of duck, hot and spicy with black beans, chilli peppers, garlic and shredded ginger.

ACKNOWLEDGEMENTS

Photography
All photographs were supplied by the
Anthony Blake Photo Library

Artists
Stonecastle Graphics

The publishers also wish to acknowledge the help given by
Kew Rendezvous
Poon's of Covent Garden

Typesetting by MS Filmsetting Limited, Frome, Somerset
Printed in Great Britain by Balding & Mansell, Wisbech, Cambridge